beginning to see

a collection of epigrams
about the problem
of living

and the freedom to be
gained through the
buddha's insight
meditation

by a. sujata

pen-art by julie wester

unity press ☯ santa cruz

revised edition published 1975
by unity press
p.o. box 1037
santa cruz
california
95061

Library of Congress Cataloging
In Publication Data
Sujata, Anagarika, 1948–
    Beginning to See
    (Mindfulness series, no.3)
    1. Buddhist meditations. 2. Epigrams, English.
I.Title.
BQ5612.S9   1974   294.3'4'43   74-8207
ISBN   0-913300-35-7
        Printed in the United States
            of America

beginning to see

much suffering
comes into the
life of one who
tries to be any-
where but
here
in the present
moment.

(here you are)

are you
content
with where you
are right now?

because "right nows" are all you have.

there is nothing
in this life that we can
have for very long...

things and people
come...

then leave us...

and we are left
sad and aching
because of
our
attachment.

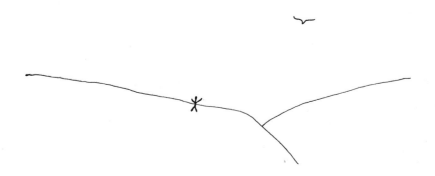

because we are only
accepting of pleasure
in our lives

an immense
amount of fear
is created, as
we spend our
lives dodging
pain.

an immense amount
of fear is created
as we spend our
lives dodging pain

an immense amount
of fear is created
as we spend our
lives dodging pain.

the world continually
demands that we
direct our
attention
OUTSIDE
ourselves.

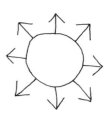

meditation teaches
us to revolt

and turn that
awareness towards
our neglected,
dimly-lit
insides...

Painful feelings
in the mind indicate
wrong attitudes
about life.

a meditation
retreat can show
us what we're
doing wrong.

we live our
lives fearfully

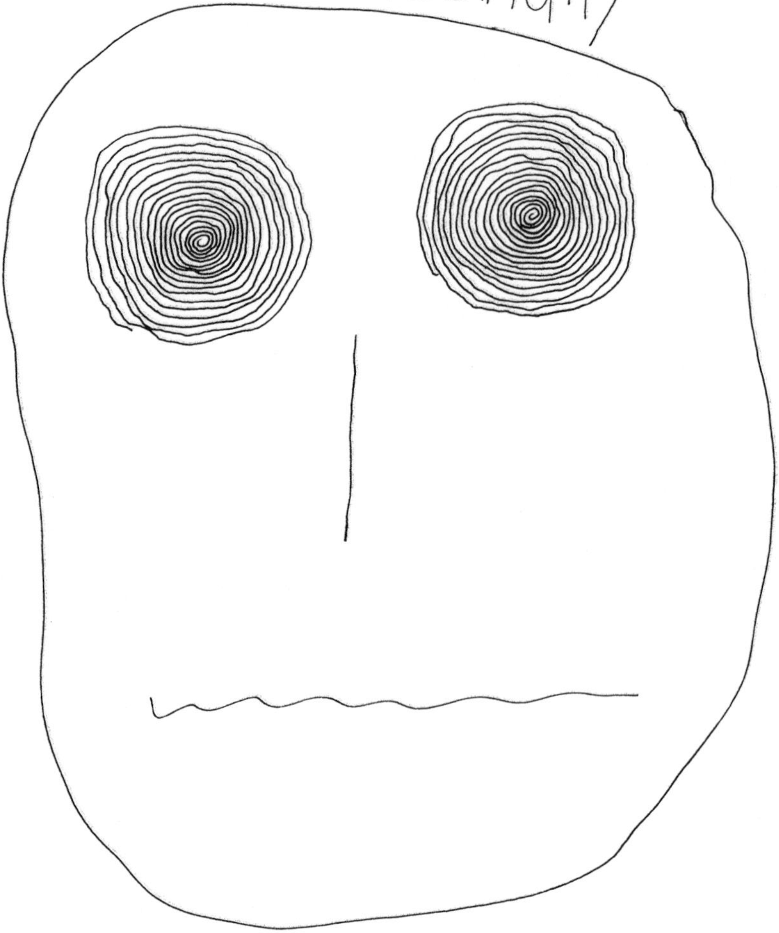

to such an extent
that we live
dishonestly.

there is dishonesty
in any mind
which demands
that reality
occur in a
specific way.

we progress in this
life according to our
honest wisdom.

honest wisdom is
realizing what you feel,
knowing what you think,
and opening
your attention
   to everything
    which comes
     before you.

We should take
time each day to
understand
ourselves...

to watch exactly
what we experience
in one hour of walk-
ing and one hour
of sitting meditation.

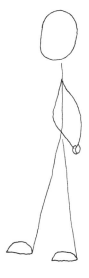

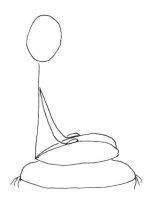

choices in a
meditator's life are
very simple :

he does those
things which contribute
to his awareness

he refrains from
things which do not.

for the enlightened
meditator life is merely
a process of experience,
then awareness, then wisdom,
then detachment, then bliss,
then lovingkindness.

the first step in
Spiritual growth is to
do what we love to do
and to become
aware of doing it.

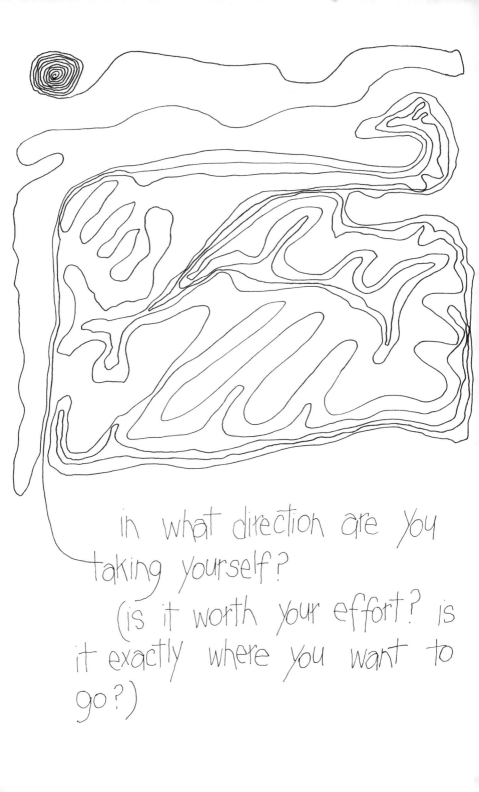

in what direction are you taking yourself?
(is it worth your effort? is it exactly where you want to go?)

the buddha taught
insight meditation
to those wise ones
who were tired of
the ups and downs
of living
and desired
lasting peace

have you ever
considered
cessation?

not suicide,
cessation.... something
very constructive

insight meditation systematically trains us to be aware of everything "we're up to."

the mind is only a
sophisticated
mirror

it is what it sees
it is what it sees

be careful what
you show it because
you can be

anything
anything
anything
anything

ego is but a worri-
some product of unmind-
ful, wandering thoughts.

when powerful awareness is
cultivated, we gladly learn
that there is
               no one who thinks—
                      only thinking

               no one who walks—
                      only walking

               no one who sees—
                      only seeing
               and finally the great
                 burden is dissolved

detached
does not mean
dead.

rather, it is made of

lovingkindness

compassion

sympathetic joy

and

equanimity

one of the
highest blessings is
a friend with whom
we can respond
openly and freely

this living is
so hard
how can we
be anything
but loving?

besides teaching insight meditation, the buddha also taught a meditation to develop loving kindness for all creatures — he instructed that we sit in a quiet place and reflect first on the dangers of hatred, anger and resentment, and the benefits of loving kindness — these reflections remind us of the importance of maintaining a loving attitude in all circumstances and give us energy for the meditation.

because only when there is love for one- self can there be love for others, we first practice loving kindness towards ourselves by thinking of our own good qualities and kind actions — warmth for ourselves grows as we repeat over and over the loving thought: 'may I be free from my troubles (anger, fear, tension, anxiety, hatred, etc.) may I live happily.'

when we first begin the practice of loving- kindness, we may be surprised to find that we have difficulty in reflecting on our good qualities — we may feel shy or guilty in thinking of ourselves in such a positive way, or there may be self-hatred conditioned in our minds by years of comparing ourselves with others or with some ideal to which we might cling.

when we begin practice, it may be help- ful to start each period of practice by writing down a few reflections to help us focus our attention.

for example, one day our reflections might be:

dangers of hatred and resentment

1- makes me fearful
2- creates restlessness and agitation
3- makes me feel miserable
4- makes me critical and hard on myself

advantages of lovingkindness

1- makes my mind clear
2- frees my body of tension
3- makes me feel good about myself
4- makes it easier to be with others

my own good qualities

1- I try to be patient
2- I am willing to change and grow
3- I want to be more loving
4- I have pretty toes

Spend some time each day writing and reflecting in this way — then spend the last ten minutes of the meditation time specifically cultivating that warm and open space which thoughts of lovingkindness produce, by gently and silently repeating your own wish for yourself: 'may I be loving,' or 'may I be free from restlessness,' or 'may I be free from anxiety,' in whatever way feels appropriate for you.

if we work ardently at this meditation, we will begin to see a healthy change happening within ourselves.

In time, when loving thoughts flow freely for ourselves, the lovingkindness may be extended to all beings everywhere without distinction—

may all beings be happy.

anger is most
dangerous.
it destroys you,
the person next
to you,
and the place where
you live.

when aversion arises in
our minds,
we must either mindfully
drop it,
or start communicating.

hatred
is a crime
   in any of its forms --
   resentment, aversion,
   jealousy, anger, harshness,
      disgust --

      if we watch carefully
what it does to our
feelings and what we do
to other people's feelings
when motivated by it, we
have no choice but to
give it up.

we are very empty inside
just watch us work to fill
up the vacant hours

time on our
hands is very
dangerous.

we might stop long
enough to notice that
we are very unhappy
people

going nowhere
special. . . . . .

the buddha did not
come in the 6th
century b.c.

to reassure us
that
the world was
moving in the
right
direction.

Once a king who was marching to war came near the place where an enlightened teacher was living. the king was in a great hurry but he wanted to learn something from the saint. respectfully the king approached, paid homage, and asked the holy one,

"will you tell me the buddha's teachings, for i have little time and may even be killed this very day."

the sage looked upon the man in the royal cloak and answered with but one word,

"awareness."

mindfully
    attending to the sensation
of the breath—
        a tranquility and
insight exercise—
        is politically, economically
        and spiritually

the practice
of
peacefulness

a vipassana meditation exercise

For the development of clear, mindful awareness, the buddha taught us to observe closely the movements of the body and the mind. a good way to develop your attentiveness, concentration and insight, is to watch carefully the rising and falling of the abdomen. In this meditation exercise we begin by observing these obvious bodily movements. When these become clear we will also be able to be aware of the more subtle movements of the mind.

go to a quiet place and sit in a comfortable position with eyes closed and back straight but not rigid. the movement of the abdomen is always present: place your attention on its natural in and out movement, making a mental note of each part of the process as it is occurring. It is not necessary to verbally repeat the words, "rising" and "falling," or even to think of "rising" and "falling" in the form of words. Instead, only be aware of the actual process of rising and falling. as you become more and more alert and can follow the movements more carefully, you will become aware that the breathing is sometimes shallow, sometimes deep, sometimes rapid, sometimes slow and calm. These variations should be noted, however there should be no effort to control or to interfere with the breathing in any way. Just choicelessly watch the movements as they appear when you are breathing normally.

While you are watching the rise and fall of the abdomen, the mind may, by itself, go towards other objects, such as thoughts, feelings, bodily sensations. These new objects should be noted as soon as they arise. If a thought comes to your mind, be aware of "thinking." If a sound comes to your attention, make a mental note of "hearing." After each such note, firmly and calmly return your attention to the primary objects of meditation, the movements of the abdomen.

As you develop more concentration on the primary objects, you will quickly notice any other object as it arises. However, until the mind is alert enough to notice these objects as soon as they arise, it will tend to wander unmindfully after these thoughts, feelings and emotions. Sometime later, the meditator becomes aware that he has been daydreaming. As soon as one is aware that his attention has drifted away from the present moment, he should patiently note that his mind has been "wandering," and that he is now "remembering to be mindful." Then one should lovingly return the attention to watching the rising and falling.

Mindfulness can also be practiced during walking meditation, with the lifting, placing and putting of the foot as the primary objects of awareness. With head upright, keeping your eyes on the ground about six feet ahead, walk at a moderately slow pace, with steps small enough so that, without losing your balance, you can place one foot firmly on the ground before moving the next foot. Remember to note each part of the movement as it occurs. It is a good idea to spend equal amounts of time in walking and in sitting meditation —— for example, thirty minutes of walking, then thirty of sitting; later, one hour of walking, then one hour of sitting.

during all movements and activities of the day —— eating, washing, moving from place to place, job to job —— one should be aware of the movements of the body necessary for each activity, or of any thought, feeling or physical sensation which arises predominately.

one who persists in noting all objects as they come to his attention will develop increasingly clear awareness. noting should be done neither too fast nor too slowly. It should be immediate, firm and clear, but not harsh. one is not to be lazy and sit daydreaming, but rather to develop an awareness of the objects which is accepting and alert. at a certain point when the mindfulness is well developed, awareness will be automatic, and there will be less and less need for making mental notes. however, whenever attention weakens, one should return to making clear notes.

it would be convenient if one could simply "decide" to be aware. however, we are conditioned not to be aware. our minds are trained to be complicated, and so it is necessary to re-train ourselves in order to be simply aware. The most skillful way for a beginning meditator to develop mindful awareness is to place himself under the guidance of a qualified meditation teacher for a period of intense practice. during a meditation retreat one leaves behind for a time the rush and trouble of his daily life, and in an atmosphere of quiet mindfulness and lovingkindness, devotes his energy entirely to the development of awareness. The minimum length of time usually needed for beginning westerners is one month. after completing such a period of intensive meditation, one is better able to continue the development and practice of mindfulness in daily life.

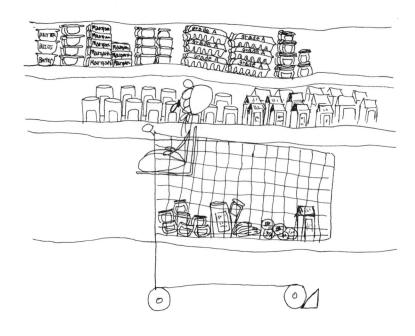

what could be
better than a
meditation you
can take
anywhere?

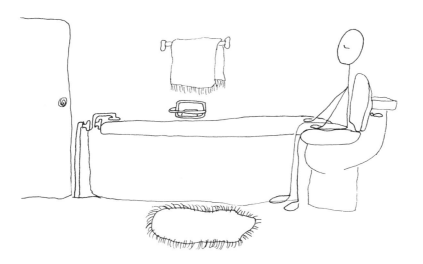

a saint is a very simple man:

when he walks, he walks.
when he talks, he talks.
and that's all.

he doesn't think while
    listening,
day dream while walking,
see while touching.

that is very hard.
that is why he is a saint.
that is why there is
trouble in our lives.

tension
is the first noble truth:

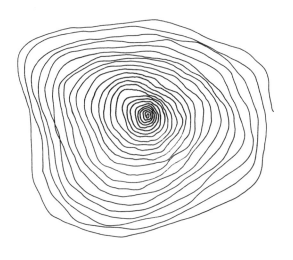

life is suffering.

the price of
wisdom
is pain:

but it is this wisdom
that cuts off
the suffering.

finally, there is
no choice but
to bleed freely.

Your pain can be
the breaking
of the shell
which
encloses

your

under-
standing.

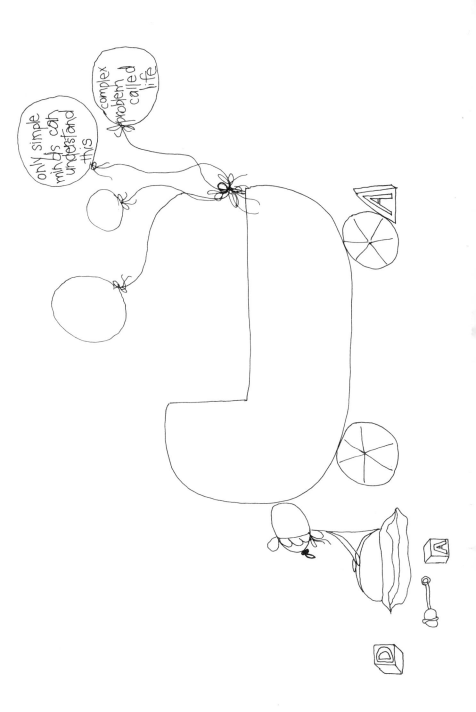

if we accept everything
in life as our
teacher

we soon will
be
     free
from the
pain of
unnecessary resistance
and
unnecessary desire.

We run here and there and there
all our lives
trying to be successful,
correct and right

when the
goal
of life
is
learning

meditation does not necessarily make us feel good, but it does awaken us to the many things we do feel...

a meditation retreat
brings great relief because
for a time we don't have
to take our mind and its
problems seriously,

we don't have to act
upon its thousand wander-
ing thoughts,

we just note them
mindfully and they pass
away . . . .

the untrained
mind is so
Vulnerable to
Circumstances

something good
happens and it
is happy...

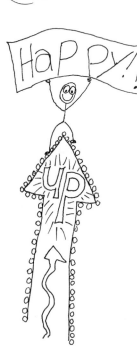

something bad
happens and it
is in pain...

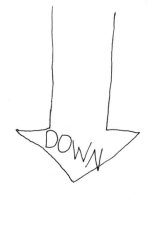

one who has sufficiently
suffered the attachments
and aversions of his mind's
uncontrolled wanderings
quickly becomes
watchful of any direction in which the mind moves...

Your mind has
a mind of its
own

(where
do
you
fit in?)

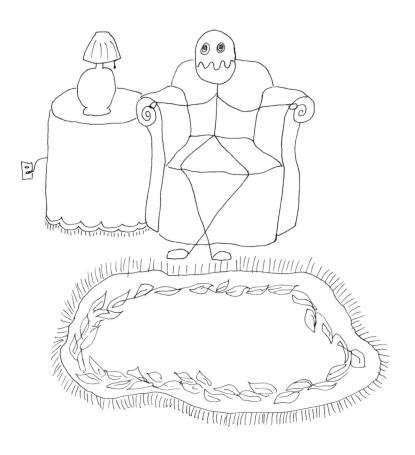

if we think the noise of traffic is loud, we should go into a quiet room and listen to our minds.

thoughts are not
necessarily connected
with reality

that is why the
buddha taught us
to be aware
of them
before we are
influenced
by them

what happens between
the time we awake
and the time we
go to bed

is out.
of our control.

bittersweet goes the life of him—
that clouded and distracted
    stranger to reality...
without awareness, he
    stumbles and falls
he hurts himself to death.

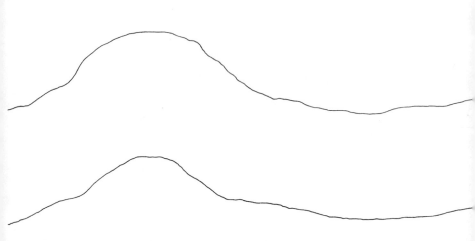

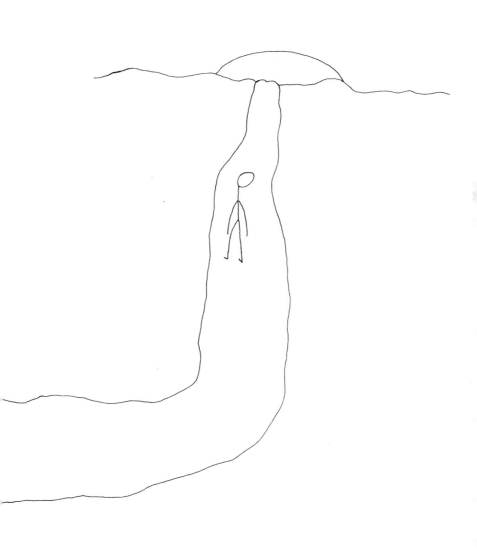

if living were an easy
thing to do
there would be no need
for mental training

but because life often
becomes very,
very hard

we often have
to meditate
very, very
hard.

the mind is the
only means we have
of getting out of
this mess.

careful
with it

immorality,
selfishness,
anger and
chemicals

dull this single key.

everyone needs
a period of mental
and physical
seclusion every day.

meditating is
   the kindest
thing we can
   do for
ourselves.

our mind is a
garden
by selecting what it thinks
upon, we can grow
either thorny weeds
or beautiful
tender flowers

(but even a
little weed
can learn
to grow
flowers)

Our characters are
developed by persistent practice

if we practice love
we become more loving

if we practice patience
we become more patient

if we practice generosity
we become more generous.

communication lovingkindness

insight into reality

form an interdependent
triangle :

neglect one and we
diminish the other two

practice one and all
are increased

basically,
life is unsatisfactory
because:

1. it is not perfect
2. we only get two weeks of vacation
   each year.
3. our joys are impermanent.
4. the coke machine won't work.
5. our bodies have to be washed over
   and over again.
6. the free way is crowded.
7. we must be taught by pain as well
   as by pleasure.
8. our name sounds dumb.
9. we must argue that life is not
   unsatisfactory.
10. most of our happiness depends
    on mere thoughts of the past
    and the future.

mindfulness is
the cure for the
disease of
suffering

Rx   Rx

mindfulness

keep within
reach of everyone.

to be wealthy
we must spend our
time making money

to be free
we must spend our
time practicing
mindfulness.

reaching
enlightenment
is just a matter
of continuous
practice . . . . ✶

omb to tomb
to womb to tom
omb to tomb to womb
to womb to tomb to wom
omb to tomb to womb to ton
mb to womb to tomb to tomb t
mb to tomb to womb to tomb to
b to womb to tomb to womb to t
to tomb to womb to tomb to womb
mb to womb to tomb to womb to tom
b to tomb to womb to tomb to womb
b tomb to womb to tomb to womb tot
mb to tomb to womb to tomb to womb
to tomb to womb to

nirvana is an
alternative
to life, after life, after
life, after life, after
life, after life, after
life, after life, after life
after life, after life, after life, after life, after life, after life, after life, after life, after life, after life, after life, after life, after life, after life, after life, after life, after

During the time of the buddha, there was a young monk called nanda who did not understand the necessity for mindfulness. one day, nanda began to cherish the idea of giving his best robe to the enlightened teacher sangara. nanda was most infatuated with the idea, thinking that it would be an act of great merit to show such generosity towards a spiritually developed being. he thought to himself, "by this noble deed, surely i will soon attain enlightenment." because he was not yet well trained to mindfully watch the nature of his thoughts, nanda did not recognize the selfish desire and attachment which made his intentions impure.

the next day the young monk waited until sangara left the monastery. in his absence, nanda swept his room, brought water for drinking and washing, prepared a seat for him of cushions and flowers, and laid out the gift of the robe. then nanda sat down and waited. when he saw sangara returning, he quickly went out to the road, greeted him respectfully, and brought him to his quarters. seeing the room, the teacher was pleased with the young monk's energy and kindness. nanda invited him to be seated on the prepared seat, gave him water to drink, bathed his feet. then nanda took a palm leaf and began to fan the holy one. he began the presentation of the gift, saying that he wanted with all his heart to give this, his best robe, to sangara.

the teacher detected that the young monk had not been mindful of his desires and had allowed himself to become attached to the idea of giving this gift. seeing this as an opportunity to teach nanda the danger of unmindfulness, the holy one replied that he already had a complete set of robes, and as he had no need for the gift, instructed nanda to give the robe to some needy monk. at this, nanda repeated his request several times, only to have the teacher thank him for offering the gift, but instruct him to give it elsewhere.

this polite refusal hurt nanda's feelings and resentment arose in his mind. in this clouded state of mind, he stood fanning the teacher. rather than practicing mindfulness by dismissing his resentment and attending to the fanning, nanda permitted his mind to dwell on the incident. as his mind wandered concerning the declined gift, his resentment grew, and he thought,

"if sangara is not willing to receive my gift, why should i remain a monk? i will become a householder once more." then his thoughts began to wander restlessly, taking his attention farther and farther from the present moment in which he stood fanning the teacher. . . . . "suppose i become a householder once more," he thought, "how shall i earn a living? i will sell this robe and buy myself a she-goat. as the she-goat brings forth young, i will sell them and in this way make a profit. when i have accumulated a profit, i will take a wife, and my wife will bear me a son. i will put my son in a little cart, and taking son and wife along with me, i will make the journey back here to pay respects to the elder sangara. as we travel, i will say to my wife, 'wife, bring me my son, for i wish to carry him.' she will reply, 'why should you carry the boy? you push the cart.' saying this, she will take the boy in her arms, thinking to carry him herself; but lacking the necessary strength, she will let him fall in the road and he will land in the path of the wheels and the cart will run over him. then i will say to her, 'wife, you have ruined me.' so saying, i will bring down my stick upon her head."

so pondered nanda as he stood fanning the elder. consumed by his reflections, he swung his palm-leaf fan and brought it down on the head of the elder. sangara considered within himself, "why has nanda struck me on the head?" immediately becoming aware of every thought which had passed through the mind of his attendant, he said to him, "nanda, you did not succeed in hitting the woman, but what has an old teacher done to deserve a beating?" the young monk thought to himself, "i am in disgrace! the elder knows all the foolish thoughts which have passed through my mind."

the teacher told nanda that if he sought forgiveness he should come and sit before him. trembling, nanda sat down, his eyes cast upon the floor he had so proudly swept a short time before.

Sangara spoke quietly and patiently, "Nanda, do you see that you have made no effort to mindfully watch your thoughts; and do you see how needlessly you have suffered because of your mind's unwatched wanderings?

"Your gift was not freely given because you demanded that it be received in a specific way. When your demands were unfulfilled you suffered resentment. The resentment was allowed to grow unwatched until it had made you completely unmindful. As you stood fanning me, you negligently became absorbed in wandering thoughts which had nothing to do with the present moment.

"Do you see now the danger of unmindful thinking? Do you see that if the mind is not carefully watched, one will become painfully absorbed in unwholesome states of mind? One unwholesome mental state weakens the mind so that it becomes susceptible to another and another. In this way, your mind, weakened by selfish desires, became caught in attachment, which led to disappointment, resentment, delusion and now regret.

"Nanda, work gently and persistently to develop the mindfulness. As you have seen, one who does not live each moment in mindful awareness is bound for one painful experience after another. He who learns to watch the restless cravings and painful attachments of the mind will soon give up the suffering."

the innocent mind is willing to try anything... just because of its innocence.

To be free we
must be comfortable
in being someone, anyone
or no one at any time
in any place.

please remember...
everything which
has a beginning
has an ending.

if we do not approach the matter of diet intelligently we will only constipate our minds. isn't freedom achieved when we can appreciatively accept any type of food that is offered?

attachment to any diet is spiritually poisonous... food in itself is not a means of transcendence. it only sustains the body while the mind works for its enlightenment.

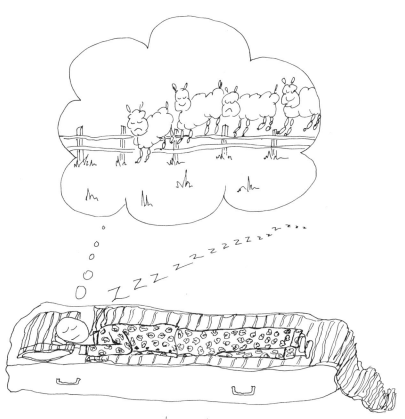

we must sleep away
one-third of our
lives because

we wear ourselves out
liking and disliking
all day long

our relationships
are unfree to the
extent that we
demand things of
other people

neurotics depend on
holidays, weekends
and days-off.

those who cultivate
their appreciation
celebrate
daily.

each morning, if we
commit ourselves to finding
the truth of every
situation
then miracles will
come to us
all day long

when you find out who
you really are
it's beautiful
beyond your
dreams

is there
anything better
to be than
free?

when you're
flying
you can talk or not talk,
   sing or not sing,
dance or not dance,
   laugh or not laugh,
eat or not eat,
   play or not play,
be serious or not be serious,
   draw a picture or not
draw a picture
touch someone or not
   touch someone

go or stay   live or die
   and it all
   tastes the same...
joyful   joyful   joyful

dear friend

i hope that this book
has taught you how very
dishonestly you
are living
your life

and how very far
you are from being
free

for this is
the most beautiful
lesson that i
have learned.

with love,
sujata

dear friend
i hope that this book
has taught you how very
innocently you
are living
your life

and how very close
you are to being
free

for this is
the most beautiful
lesson that i
have learned.

with love,
sujata

believe nothing
merely because you have been
told it, or because it is
traditional, or because you
yourself have imagined it. do
not believe what your teacher
tells you, merely out of respect
for the teacher.

but whatever way by
thorough examination you find
to be one leading to good and
happiness for all creatures,

that path follow, like the
moon in the path
of stars

an american who began his search for understanding at a young age, sujata traveled half-way around the world where he found some very rare people who, unlike all others he had met, were not plagued by the universal human enslavements of hatred, attachment and selfishness. using the tools of satipatthana vipassana meditation which he practiced as a buddhist monk, sujata teaches meditators to watch carefully the ways of the mind. as resident teacher of stillpoint institute, he guides others along the path of dhamma, through the difficult process of laying down the burden of "self."

for more information about the practice of vipassana (insight) meditation and mindful awareness, you may read:

The Experience of Insight: a natural unfolding
   by joseph goldstein

and Living Buddhist Masters
   by jack kornfield

both available from
   Unity Press
   P.O. Box 1037
   Santa Cruz,
   California 95061.

for information about intensive meditation retreats you may contact
   Stillpoint Institute
   604 South 15th Street
   San Jose,
   California 95112
   Telephone: (408)-287-5307.